Love Is an Orientation

Participant's Guide

Participant's Guide

Love Is an Orientation

Practical Ways to
Build Bridges with
the Gay Community

SIX SESSIONS

Andrew Marin
with Ginny Olson

ZONDERVAN®

ZONDERVAN.com/
AUTHORTRACKER
follow your favorite authors

ZONDERVAN

Love Is an Orientation Participant's Guide
Copyright © 2011 by Andrew Marin

Requests for information should be addressed to:
Zondervan, *Grand Rapids, Michigan 49530*

ISBN 978-0-310-89127-7

Cover design: Cindy Kiple
Cover photography: Duncan Walker/iStockphoto (grunge paper); Nick Pardo/Getty Images (three males walking)
Interior design: Sherri L. Hoffman

Printed in the United States of America

11 12 13 14 15 16 17 18 /DCI/ 20 19 18 17 16 15 14 13 12 11 10 9 8 7 6 5 4 3 2 1

Contents

Contents

Introduction

Welcome to the participant's guide for the *Love Is an Orientation* video curriculum. Learning to be a bridge builder, by seeking productive dialogue through relationship and reconciliation between two separated communities, will be one of the most difficult commitments of your life. It's so hard because in many situations it's just not satisfying. Your time might be filled with discomfort, pressure, confusion, and heavy burdens you don't know how you'll carry; and yet, you will simultaneously know the ultimate joy of what it means to invest into a kingdom that the Lord so longs to bring to our world here and now.

Rooted at or near the center of the constant social unrest and political culture wars that cover our landscape today seems to be the disconnect between the lesbian, gay, bisexual, and transgender (LGBT) community, evangelicals, and conservatives in general. Each group has become subhuman to the other; a mere voting bloc that is preyed on and pressured by extreme activism tearing the fabric of our churches and government apart. It's our time, right now, to step up and lead our culture forward by practicing what it means to build bridges among division, letting our surrounding world know that impact and authority are earned through those who know what it means to have love as their orientation.

I humbly pray that as you engage this curriculum, the Spirit of the Lord might permeate each session and discussion time; that you might feel empowered to do what so many others will

never have the courage to do—intentionally immerse yourself
in the most theologically and politically divisive topic in our
culture today and be known by your love.

Andrew Marin
Boystown, Chicago
September 2011

How to Use This Study

Homosexuality is one of the most divisive issues in the global church today and people usually are firmly planted on one side of the rift or the other. The result is two diverse communities, often at odds. The *Love Is an Orientation* video curriculum is designed to assist churches, universities, seminaries, nonprofits, government agencies, and discussion groups discover how to build bridges across this rift with the lesbian, gay, bisexual, and transgender (LGBT) community. Increasing numbers have expressed a desire to understand and love their LGBT neighbors, but have lacked either the knowledge or the experience to engage in the bridge-building process.

Love Is an Orientation is based on Andrew Marin's award-winning book of the same name (InterVarsity Press, 2009), as well as the work of The Marin Foundation, a nonprofit organization that since 2005 has sought to build bridges between the LGBT community and the church "through scientific research, biblical and social education, and diverse community gatherings" (*www.themarinfoundation.org*).

As a participant in this curriculum, there may be times when you will be challenged to go beyond your comfort level and other times when you may or may not agree with everything said on the video. The hope is that you will continue to move through places of discomfort and become a bridge builder for the sake of Christ.

Format of the *Love Is an Orientation* Curriculum

The curriculum is divided into six hour-long sessions. Each session includes:

Starter Question

The starter question is intended to orient your thinking toward the session topic. You may decide to answer the question as a group at the beginning of the discussion time *or* you may wish to reflect on the question prior to the group gathering.

Video Teaching Session

During the video, you are encouraged to follow along or take notes using the basic outline printed in this participant's guide. (Session videos average 23 minutes.)

Video Discussion

Following the video are several questions to help facilitate the discussion of the material and also to help you reflect and act on what you are learning.

Scripture Discussion

Next, you will explore one of the Scripture passages presented in the video (or other passages related to the topic).

Wrap-Up

If your group has time, please view one of the stories on the Real Stories section of the DVD. (These bonus videos vary in length from 7–11 minutes.)

The session ends with a concluding thought or prayer suggestion. Discussion about a topic such as homosexuality can be very personal and generate numerous emotions. Use this time to check in with each other and make sure everyone feels at least some degree of closure. Perhaps it would be appropriate to pray for someone or apologize to someone at this time.

Next Steps

Each session features action steps to continue the learning process between meetings. Consider discussing the results of the previous week's efforts during each group gathering. Or you may choose to keep a journal of your next steps. Discussions are important, but never let them take the place of active living, learning, and implementation in your everyday life and local community.

Glossary

The following is a short list of terms, with simple definitions, which are used in this participant's guide and the video. For more terms and fuller definitions, see the websites listed in Appendix A beginning on page 87.

Bisexual: A person who is attracted physically or romantically to both women and men.

Gay: A self-identified man who is physically or romantically attracted to the same sex. It can refer exclusively to men or be used as an overarching term for both men and women who are attracted to the same sex.

Homosexual: While referring to people who are attracted to those of the same sex, this term is seen as derogatory and should be avoided. Use "gay," "lesbian," or another appropriate term, such as LGBT.

LGBT: The most current and commonly accepted acronym signifying lesbian, gay, bisexual, and transgender persons. GLBT is also a common alternative and the one that Andrew used in the original *Love Is an Orientation* book. Other less common alternatives are: LGBTQ, with "Q" denoting "queer" or "questioning"; LGBTI with "I" signifying "intersex "; or LGBT* with the asterisk representing several other labels.

Lesbian: A woman who self-identifies as physically or romantically attracted to the same sex. They can also be referred to as "gay women."

Intersex: A person who is born with a sexual or reproductive anatomy that is neither typically male nor female. This person may choose to identify as being either male or female.

Queer: While historically an offensive word, it is currently rising in popularity in some LGBT circles as an overarching descriptive term. However, it is still deemed as pejorative when used by straight people.

Sexual Orientation: Used to describe a person's physical or romantic attraction to the same or other sex or both.

Straight: A casual term describing a self-identified person (or group) physically or romantically attracted to the other, or opposite, sex. Formal term: "heterosexual."

Transgender: A broad term used to describe someone whose gender identity varies from his or her biological sex. People who identify as transgender usually feel as if they have been born into the body of the "wrong" gender. Example: they may have male anatomies but feel that their gender identity is female.

Love Is Our Orientation

Many Christians see a GLBT person's "out and proud" status and automatically group that individual into a broad category of God-hating militants. To begin this journey of building bridges, however, we need to put ourselves, as much as heterosexual Christians can, into the cloudy circumstances and daily life of what it is to live attracted to people of the same sex.

(*Love Is an Orientation*, p. 23)

Starter Question —————————————————————

Describe a time when you knew someone loved you, whether you felt like you deserved it or not. What did they do that communicated love? How did that experience impact you?

Video Teaching Session #1————————

Use the following outline to follow along with the video or take notes if you wish.

Love must be our orientation.

Inward perspective

Reminder: "Love the sinner; hate the sin," versus, "Love the sinner; hate the sin in our own lives."

Reminder: "Right from the gate, I can't relate."

Power and privilege

Be a servant, a listener, and a learner first.

Outward interaction: building bridges

    False models of the ideal situation

    Difference between validation and affirmation

Cultural reconciliation versus biblical reconciliation

Live and love in real time.

Video Discussion

1. Andrew observes in the video presentation that if you are a straight person, "right from the gate, you can't relate." If we can't relate, then we must become learners. On a scale from 1–5 (1 being unwilling, 5 being eager), how willing are you to learn about someone who is gay? How willing are you to learn about gay culture?

   If you lean toward the 1 end of the scale, what is causing you to hesitate about this learning process?

   If you lean toward the 5 end of the scale, what inspires you about this learning process?

2. If you have ever done so, describe a time when you sat down with someone who is LGBT and listened to their story. Without revealing names, what did you learn about them? What did you learn about yourself?

3. What do you think a biblical reconciliation with LGBT people might look like in your church? If you were to switch perspectives, would an LGBT person agree with your description of reconciliation? Why or why not?

4. We can sometimes be attacked for engaging people who are different than we are. When that happens, Andrew says, we must genuinely work to love our enemies. Explain how you will seek to live at peace with those who might consider you the enemy if you try to build a bridge. How might you be attacked?

How will you show love toward them?

LEADER TIP

In Session 1, Andrew talks about validating each other's stories. Set a culture in your group of validating each others' stories. See the Leader Tips in Appendix C for ideas of how to do this.

This first session may be awkward or emotional or volatile or intriguing.

Scripture Discussion ——————————————————

1. Read aloud 1 John 3:23: *"And this is his command: to believe in the name of his Son, Jesus Christ, and to love one another as he commanded us."* Imagine that a lesbian couple started attending your church on a regular basis. Explain what it would mean to love them as the Lord commanded us. What are three things you would do or say to the couple to try to communicate God's love to them?

   Put yourself in the shoes of the couple. Do you think they would agree these three things communicate God's love? Why or why not?

2. Colossians 4:5–6 says, *"Be wise in the way you act toward outsiders; make the most of every opportunity. Let your conversation be always full of grace, seasoned with salt, so that you may know how to answer everyone."* Paul is giving the Christians in Colossae some sage advice on how to interact with those who aren't from their community. Historically, would you say the church has been wise or unwise in its actions toward the LGBT community?

How can your church make the most of every opportunity in its interactions with LGBT people in your community? Are these actions that will be described as wise by the LGBT community? Why or why not?

When you think of a potential conversation with an LGBT person, what might a dignified conversation that is "full of grace" sound like? What kind of questions would you ask?

How will you seek to communicate love, respect, and transparency as you talk with an LGBT person?

3. In the video, Andrew mentions Jesus' interaction with the Roman centurion (Matthew 8:5–13 or Luke 7:1–10) as an example of biblical reconciliation: "Jesus is the hinge: he came, died, rose again to reconcile God to human and human to human."

   The Romans were the ruling occupiers of Israel at the time of Jesus. They were the ones with the power. But the centurion realized his power wasn't enough to heal his servant. As a Jewish man in that culture, Jesus didn't have much perceived power. Yet the centurion knew differently. He was willing to lay down his power because he needed Jesus. Jesus' response to this interaction was, *"Truly I tell you, I have not found anyone in Israel with such great faith"* (Matthew 8:10).

Describe the power you have, either individually or culturally.

How willing are you to put aside your power in order to be reconciled to someone who is LGBT, and how will you go about living intentionally past the power structures culture has dictated?

How might Philippians 2:3 – 4 — *"Do nothing out of selfish ambition or vain conceit. Rather, in humility value others above yourselves, not looking to your own interests but each of you to the interests of the others"* — affect how you think about this?

Wrap-Up

An essential component of learning how to love is learning how to listen. If your group has time, complete your study by opening your heart and listening to one of the stories from the Real Stories section on the DVD.

Then go around the group and ask each person to tell one insight or action step they will take away from this session. Pray for each other and the stories that you heard as you shared.

Next Steps

Choose one of the following steps to further explore the session topic or to act on what you've learned. You may want to keep a journal of the steps you take, or discuss them in your next group gathering.

1. Brainstorm some ideas of what your community could do to engage in bridge-building activities between conservatives and LGBTs.

2. Name one thing you will do this week to learn about LGBT people or their culture. Here are some ideas to get you started:

   • Visit one of the websites under the heading in Appendix A that feels least like you (e.g., if you consider yourself conservative, visit a site under the heading "Progressive").

   • Read about the history of LGBT people in the United States.

   • Read an LGBT news outlet online, for example, the *Windy City Times, Washington Blade, Metro Weekly, 365gay.com, Frontiers LA*, or the *Advocate*.

- Ask an LGBT person if they would be willing to share their story with you over coffee. Take care to listen and ask open-ended questions. No preaching allowed. *And pay for the coffee.*

3. Read the following Scriptures. Ask God to give you ideas of how to apply each passage to building a bridge with the LGBT community.

    - Proverbs 16:7
    - Matthew 5:43–48
    - Luke 6:27–36
    - Philippians 2:3–4
    - 1 Timothy 4:15

Building Bridges

Until the body of Christ believes that peaceful productivity with gays and lesbians is actually an option, how can we ever expect it to happen? This is the first main step to how Christians begin to elevate the conversation past a street fight. It's a lot like the first step God commanded Joshua to take into the flooded Jordan River before the Israelites could cross into the Promised Land (Joshua 3). Take a small, yet difficult and uncertain step with the Lord toward another person — even with a very real feeling of overwhelming trepidation for what might happen — and just watch what happens as that little step inaugurates life-altering redemptive conversations about the things of God with the GLBT community.

(*Love Is an Orientation*, p. 80)

Starter Question

Faithfulness is often connected with trustworthiness and steadfastness. When someone is faithful, we know we can count on him or her, even when times are difficult. When people are faithful, you can trust them with your story, with your journey, and with your life because you know they will continue to be there for you. Describe a relationship that may not be "successful" in the world's terms, or even the church's terms, but where someone proved to be faithful in difficult circumstances. What were the ramifications of that faithfulness?

"Most people within the GLBT community who are threatened by traditional interpretations of the Bible as it pertains to homosexuality want nothing to do with it—and by extension, anyone who embraces it. How can Christians build a bridge in that circumstance?"

(*Love Is an Orientation*, p. 154)

Video Teaching Session #2 ——————————————

Use the following outline to follow along with the video or take notes if you wish.

Faithfulness is the new evangelism.

Faithfulness and success and the kingdom of God

Desirable outcomes

"Go to all the nations."

This includes the LGBT community.

"The Great Commission may not be the great reality."

Engaging culture in order to build bridges

"Their"

Jesus chose to go to the people rather than waiting for the people to come to him.

A changing metric

Joshua and the Jordan River

Video Discussion

1. In the video, Andrew talks about the need to change the paradigm from a goal of trying to "win" people to Christ to one of faithfulness. In what ways do you agree or disagree with this idea?

> "Christians have been assigned to live out our faithfulness to God by reaching across and responding to all social and spiritual issues in such a way that follows God's ideal on how to live as a distinctive follower."
>
> (*Love Is an Orientation*, p. 153)

2. Why do you think faithfulness is such an important quality to have as you build bridges with the LGBT community?

3. Imagine that your neighbor, who is gay, invites you over to his and his partner's home for a dinner party. How would you respond to the invitation? If you say yes, what's your level of comfort or discomfort?

How will you seek to be a bridge-building neighbor in this situation?

4. What would you like your church to be known for when it comes to the LGBT community? What needs to happen for that to occur?

Scripture Discussion

1. Throughout the Scriptures, we see that an attribute of God, which is frequently praised, is faithfulness. Explore Joshua 3 and take note of how Joshua was faithful to God.

   How, in turn, was God faithful to Joshua and the Israelites?

   The Israelite priests had to step out in faith. What is a step God might be asking you to take in regard to the LGBT community?

2. Faithfulness isn't just between God and us. Faithfulness also needs to be exemplified between people. In 3 John 5–8, John talks about how a particular Christian (Gaius) put his faithfulness into action toward strangers. What was the result of his faithfulness?

John suggests that the motivation for showing hospitality to others should be so that we can work together for truth. Caution: Sometimes we, as Christians, can think that our job is to just present "truth" without engaging in relationships. Andrew addresses the dangers of this in his book:

> Christians tend to perceive themselves as morally superior to GLBT people, based on the belief that the Bible allows only three options for connecting faith and sexuality: be heterosexual, be celibate or live in sin. Once Christians have presented these three options to a gay person, most consider their job effectively complete as it's now up to the gay person to either embrace or reject this truth. Yet gays and lesbians hear these three options as a definitive challenge, and therefore feel their only recourse is to suit up for battle. When it comes to identity, sexual behavior and sexuality, gays and lesbians have a unique filtration system. Our understanding of change, celibacy and sin is oppressive and destructive when run through their filter. Much of the time GLBT people just write off the rest of the conversation, and thus what began as a potentially intriguing conversation ends up as a heated debate."

(Love Is an Orientation, p. 36)

How does the excerpt from the book shed light on the passage in 3 John?

3. Hebrews 13:2 says, *"Do not forget to show hospitality to strangers, for by so doing some people have shown hospitality to angels without knowing it."* What does it mean to be hospitable to strangers? What if those strangers are lesbian, gay, bisexual, and transgender?

"A flesh-and-blood representation of Jesus Christ becomes Christianity's most effective form of building trust, forming that common ground in a belief that there is something more powerful out there petitioning our life."

(*Love Is an Orientation*, p. 154)

Wrap-Up

If your group has time, watch another story from the Real Stories section of the DVD.

As you finish this session, write down any specific plans or ideas that came to mind regarding your future interactions with someone from the LGBT community. Perhaps you sensed God prompting you to take a specific step of faith. Then spend some time doing as Proverbs 16:3 suggests — committing your plans to God that they might be established.

Next Steps

Choose one of the following steps to further explore the session topic or to act on what you've learned. You may want to keep a journal of the steps you take, or discuss them in your next group gathering.

1. Stop in a restaurant, coffee shop, community center, or bookstore in a predominantly LGBT neighborhood. Start up a conversation with some of the patrons. Find out what the neighborhood issues are. If you're not aware of such a neighborhood in your area, find a local LGBT group and do the same.

2. Visit an LGBT-affirming church or faith community. Talk to the pastor and discover the needs of his or her community. Ask if there are any books he or she would recommend or events you could attend to help you understand the LGBT community.

3. Host a focused potluck dinner with a mix of straight and gay people. Have them tell as much of their stories as they're comfortable telling. Prepare some open-ended questions in case the group needs prompting.

Theology of Bridge Builders

The Christian community has only ever known one way to handle same-sex sexual behavior: take a stand and keep a distance. Productive dialogue comes from cognitive insight and can only be accomplished through an incarnational posture of humility and living as a learner.

(*Love Is an Orientation*, p. 37)

Starter Question————————————————————————

When you discuss homosexuality with other Christians, what are the theological points that typically come up in the conversation?

Video Teaching Session #3 ———————

Use the following outline to follow along with the video or take notes if you wish.

Engaging the topic

Kingdom principles: transgenerational and transcultural

Elevating the conversation: a new starting point to talk about divisive issues

Hermeneutical approach

Book

Chapter

Verse

Word

Genesis 19: Lot's wife

Progressive point of view (Ezekiel 16:49)

Conservative point of view

Kingdom principle perspective (Luke 17:32–33)

How can we engage different world views through kingdom principles?

Video Discussion ─────────────────────────────

1. Discussion around theology can easily turn heated, as anyone who's had an argument about religion over Thanksgiving dinner can testify. Different theological perspectives are at the crux of the debate between the LGBT and theologically conservative communities. In light of that, it's important that we reflect on our theological biases as we enter into bridge building.

   Do you tend to see Scripture as word-perfect and divinely inspired, as good principles to abide by, or somewhere in between?

   How does your view of Scripture affect how you discuss theological issues with an LGBT person?

"The GLBT community sees objections to homosexuality by evangelical Christians as a form of unjust religious bigotry. The GLBT community has battled their way to what they know of religious freedom.... The best way to take gay Christians seriously is to presume that the Word of God is being taken in truthful reverence."

(*Love Is an Orientation*, p. 73)

2. In what areas might you disagree with someone who holds a different theological interpretation of homosexuality?

3. If you were discussing theology and Scripture with an LGBT person or someone else whose interpretation does not align with yours, how would you go about elevating the conversation?

4. Identify at least three kingdom principles in Scripture that can be used as you start to build bridges with others in your community. After listing them, spend some time evaluating each one. Would they differ if you were engaging LGBTs in your community?

	Kingdom Principles in Scripture	*Your Evaluation*
Example:	In Psalm 72:4 we see that God will *"defend the afflicted among the people and save the children of the needy; he will crush the oppressor."*	Do you find this principle throughout Scripture? Does it apply across genders? Across cultures?
1.		

continued on next page

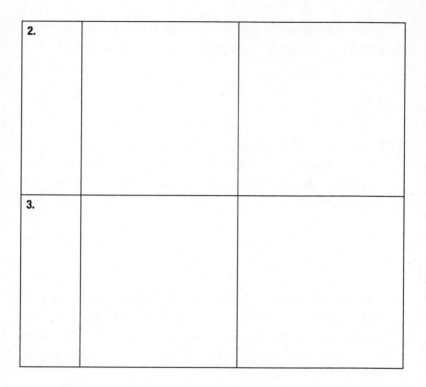

5. In the book *Love Is an Orientation*, Andrew makes the following observation:

> [Heterosexual Christians] have no problem wrestling with apologetics for people of different ethnicities and cultures that are totally removed from ours. Christians diligently study other belief systems and incarnationally move into the neighborhoods of people with different beliefs, join their groups, attend their events and partake in their daily life, reveling in the unique opportunity to engage what we don't know. But Christians do none of those things for the GLBT community.

(p.37)

Do you agree or disagree with this observation? Discuss how you arrived at your conclusion.

Four Steps to Interpret God's Word

1. What did the text mean to the biblical audience?
2. What are the cultural, language, situational, time, and covenant differences between the biblical audience and Christians today?
3. What is the overarching principle in the text?
4. How are Christians today able to best apply the overarching theological principle in their lives?

(*Love Is an Orientation*, p. 116, citing *Grasping God's Word* by J. Scott Duvall and J. Daniel Hays)

Scripture Discussion ——————————————

1. Five passages in Scripture talk specifically about homosexuality:

   - Genesis 19
   - Leviticus 18:22; 20:13
   - Romans 1:26–27
   - 1 Corinthians 6:9–11
   - 1 Timothy 1:9–11

   In the video, Andrew explores one of these passages (Genesis 19), which talks about Lot's wife. In studying it, he cites Ezekiel 16:49 and then Luke 17:32–33, which both refer to Genesis 19.

   Following that same pattern, choose one of the other four passages and explore other Scripture passages that reference the passage you selected, either directly or indirectly.

   Continuing on with the passage you selected, describe a kingdom principle that might be applicable.

2. John 4:1–42 gives us an example of Jesus having a theological conversation with someone who is from a different community. In this passage, we see Jesus deliberately choosing to take his disciples through Samaria—a land whose people had a history of conflict with the Jews. Not only did Jesus break cultural norms by traveling through Samaria, he broke gender and religious norms by engaging a woman in conversation. He was being governed by a deeper purpose: he had a love for this person and sought to build a bridge with her and her people.

What steps does Jesus take to build a bridge with the Samaritan woman?

How did Jesus elevate the conversation when it turned to theology?

What was the reaction of his disciples to their interaction?

If you choose to build bridges with people who are lesbian, gay, bisexual, and transgender, what might be the reaction of those in your church or community?

If it is a negative reaction, how will you proceed?

3. In Acts 17, we see two examples of Paul discussing faith issues with other communities. How does he elevate the conversation?

What lessons can we learn from his interactions with the Thessalonians and the Greeks?

Wrap-Up

If your group has time, watch another story from the Real Stories section of the DVD.

When it comes to homosexuality, most tend to want to debate first and build relationships later (if ever). This is not only the wrong view of engaging culture and relationships, it's also extremely detrimental to building bridges. The lasting anger, disgust, and shame that usually follow the constant back-and-forth arguing of who is politically, culturally, and theologically correct only further ingrains the rift between LGBTs and conservatives. Too many LGBT people have been wounded by the church, whether on purpose or not. As you commit to venture into the bridge-building arena, think about how you can change the ways you act, react, and interact when it comes to this divisive topic. Spend time praying about how you can start to seek reconciliation and healing. It is time to humbly turn to God for wisdom and discernment as you enter into this process. And then be encouraged and bold enough to take that step forward!

Next Steps

Choose one of the following steps to further explore the session topic or to act on what you've learned. You may want to keep a journal of the steps you take, or discuss them at your next group gathering.

1. What outlets does your group, church, university, seminary, or nonprofit offer an LGBT person when it comes to spiritual exploration and development? If nothing is currently available, what can you create in this area?
2. Create a service of lament and healing or lament and repentance for your group or congregation. This is an

opportunity to grieve over the way the church may have intentionally, or unintentionally, hurt the LGBT community. You may want to involve artists and worship leaders in this process.

3. Read chapter 5, "Gay Versus Christian and Gay Christians," in *Love Is an Orientation*. In what ways does understanding different worldviews and belief systems alter your approach to dialoguing with LGBT people?

4. Is there an LGBT person from your past whom you may need to contact and apologize to for your behavior toward him or her? Take some time this week to call or write a note.

Resource

Grasping God's Word by J. Scott Duvall and J. Daniel Hays (Zondervan, 2005).

Answering Tough Questions

One cannot work within the GLBT community without facing the tough questions that are on the tip of everyone's mind—is homosexuality right or wrong; nature or nurture; sin or non-sin; "out and proud" or ex-gay? The purpose of elevating the conversation is not to answer those questions for you, but rather to give you the framework for gays and lesbians to answer those questions with you by their side.

(*Love Is an Orientation*, p. 83)

Starter Question

When was the first time you saw an LGBT person portrayed either on television or in a movie? Do you recall the name of the movie/TV show and how they were portrayed?

Video Teaching Session #4 ————————

Use the following outline to follow along with the video or take notes if you wish.

Imputed cultural perceptions

Six main questions surrounding faith and sexuality:

1. Is someone born gay?

2. Is being gay a sin?

3. Can someone change their sexual orientation?

4. Can someone be gay and Christian?

5. Are gay people going to hell?

6. Would you vote for gay marriage?

Closed-ended versus open-ended questions

Three results of responding to close-ended questions:

1. I know who you are.

2. I know what you believe.

3. I know how I should treat you based on your one-word answer.

Theories on why we ask closed-ended questions

Jesus and close-ended questions

Jesus and the three-step approach of responding:

1. Refused to answer the question with a one-word, yes-or-no response.

2. Elevated his response to a broader kingdom principle that was applicable to everyone.

3. Took the kingdom principle and drove it home to make it relevant.

The possible result of not responding to closed-ended questions

Examples of not responding to closed-ended questions

"Closed-ended questions don't cultivate dialogue. The asker has already answered the question for themselves and is only seeking to figure out where the other person fits within their own preconceived metric — either for or against."

(Love Is an Orientation, p. 104)

Video Discussion ──────────────────────

1. As you were growing up, what were you taught about homosexuality by your church and by your family?

   Have your views changed over the years? If so, how?

   What has influenced your current beliefs about homosexuality (for example, interaction with an LGBT family member, coworker, or friend; attendance at a Bible study)? What has been your journey in landing at your current beliefs?

2. Describe a conversation you've had with either an LGBT person or someone who holds a pro-gay perspective that went well. What was it about the conversation that was positive?

Describe a conversation you've had with either an LGBT person or someone who holds a pro-gay perspective that didn't go well. In retrospect, what would you do differently?

3. In the video presentation, Andrew lists the six most frequently cited questions in today's culture war conversations surrounding faith and homosexuality. Develop at least one open-ended question that elevates the conversation in response to each of the six questions, and then discuss your questions with the group.

Scripture Discussion ————————————

Let's examine two examples of when Jesus was asked closed-ended questions.

1. In Matthew 12, Jesus is having an ongoing interaction with the Pharisees about the Sabbath. In verses 9–14, he enters onto *their* turf—the synagogue. As you read about the exchange, reflect on what Andrew said about how Jesus responds to closed-ended questions.

   What was the closed-ended question the Pharisees asked?

   What was their purpose in asking the question?

   Remember that kingdom principles are applicable across cultures and generations. What is the kingdom principle Jesus is using in his response?

   How is this kingdom principle relevant to us? What about to those in the LGBT community?

But What About ...?

Sometimes people cite 1 Peter 3:15 as a reason for giving a closed-ended answer to a closed-ended question. Take a look at not only verse 15, but also the verses that surround it (vv. 13–17). Sometimes, we can forget to respond to direct questions with gentleness and respect. The most divisive topic in our church and surrounding culture today deserves more dignity than a one-word, closed-ended answer. And don't miss that this passage addresses the question of what is the source of our hope, not what are our views on gay marriage, or homosexuality and church leadership. Not everyone is going to agree with your theological, social, or political positions. We must remember that the more time intentionally invested into sustainable, peaceful, and productive dialogue, the more one starts to look at you as a person and not a position.

2. Another example of when Jesus was asked a closed-ended question is in Matthew 19. This time the topic is eternal life and Jesus is discussing it with a man as the disciples listen.

   Reflecting on Matthew 19:16–22, what was the closed-ended question the man asked?

   What were the kingdom principles Jesus addressed in his response?

How does Jesus make it relevant to the man?

How is this principle relevant to our current culture and generation?

As Andrew mentions in the video, when we engage in dialogue with open-ended questions, drama often ensues. What was the drama that resulted from this interaction in Matthew? Consider both the man's response and the disciples' response.

NOTE: If you're interested in other times Jesus was asked closed-ended questions, read the section beginning on page 178 of *Love Is an Orientation*.

3. Jesus posed a question to his disciples in Matthew 16:13–20: *"Who do people say the Son of Man is?"* There were several layers to that question, one of which was to discover his disciples' personal perceptions regarding his identity. The first time Jesus asked the question, there was a group response (verse 14). When Jesus pushed further (verse 15), asking them to own their perspectives, only Peter answered.

Why do you think the others may not have responded?

In a situation like this, do you resonate more with Peter or with the other disciples? Do you tend to keep quiet or to speak up? (For those who tend to be quiet, know that it's not always a bad thing; just a few verses later, Peter's tendency to speak up got him in trouble.)

If an LGBT person asked you a variation of that question, "Who does God say that I am?" how would you respond? Is there an open-ended question that comes to mind?

"Open-ended questions ... require not only thought but responsiveness. A great open-ended question is, "What's it like to be you?" Such a question owns the reality that heterosexual people can never fully identify with the life experience of gay people. We take the position of the eager audience. This automatically puts us in a humbled state of listening and learning."

(*Love Is an Orientation*, p. 163)

Wrap-Up

If your group has time, watch another story from the Real Stories section of the DVD.

One statement that evangelical Christians often make is, "But I have to tell them the truth!" especially in regard to conversations with LGBT people. We tend to think God will work if we make a declaration and leave it at that. That "drop a grenade and run" tactic doesn't work. Throughout the Bible, we see evidence of God desiring to reason and dialogue with his people. Pray for opportunities to have conversations that reflect the nature of God, where we listen more than talk, where we love more than judge.

Next Steps

Choose one of the following steps to further explore the session topic or to act on what you've learned. You may want to keep a journal of the steps you take, or discuss them in your group gathering.

1. Develop some open-ended questions you could use as you engage in conversation surrounding this culturally and politically divisive topic.
2. Read one of the Gospels and make a list of the closed-ended questions Jesus was asked. Examine how he responded to each question and why.
3. Read one of the Gospels and study how Jesus' counter-cultural responses to closed-ended questions had a cultural, religious, or political impact on those he was addressing. Do you notice any patterns in people's reactions? What lessons can you learn and how do they relate to bridge building?

Adolescents and Sexuality

Research now reports that the average age of someone who first real-izes a same-sex attraction is thirteen years old. It also shows that the average age of someone who declares their sexual orientation as gay, lesbian, bisexual or transgender is fifteen years old! Think back to when you were thirteen, fourteen, and fifteen years old and add onto those already insecure, awkward years the extra burden of having these new, sometimes frightful sexual thoughts and not knowing where they came from. Who do you tell? ... The risk is just too big, and therefore most kids don't tell anyone.

(*Love Is an Orientation*, p. 23)

Starter Question —————————————————

What challenges might an LGBT adolescent face if he or she came out in the places, groups, and environments that you belong? What about at your local middle school or high school?

Video Teaching Session #5 ————————————

Use the following outline to follow along with the video or take notes if you wish.

LGBT adolescents

Questions and struggles LGBT adolescents face

Messages the church sends our adolescents

Create a ministry environment that is hospitable and safe.

What to do when an adolescent comes out to you.

A holy moment

Understand your response is important.

You're representing Jesus in this moment.

This isn't about you.

Go with them when they have difficult conversations with their family or loved ones.

A ministry should reflect James 2–3.

Bullying and LGBT adolescents

Advocating for adolescents in the community

Video Discussion

1. What messages does your church send to children and adolescents about being lesbian, gay, bisexual, or transgender?

2. On a scale from 1 to 5 (1 being very unsafe—where they would be teased and maybe ostracized, to 5 being very safe—where they would be welcomed and have a support network), how would your church rate as a safe place for an LGBT child or adolescent to worship and to enter into a journey of figuring out their faith and sexuality?

   What steps can you take to make your church a safe place?

3. If an LGBT adolescent asked you if God loved them, how would you respond?

If they asked you if God made a mistake in creating them gay, how would you respond?

1. Adults tend to want to preach at adolescents and children by automatically asserting a dominant role. It is important that group participants continue to have an attitude of learning and not judging when dealing with teenagers. There is nothing more powerful in a youth's mind than an adult who is eager to listen and learn as the youth lets them into their unique experiences, instead of the adult just trying to fix everything.

2. Be aware that it is likely that a group participant has a family member who is LGBT. You may need to revisit your group's policy on confidentiality.

3. Be prepared for "holy moments," as Adam McLane called them, as people may open up about their own adolescence or the journeys of family members. As the leader, seek to read the emotional climate of the group. Sometimes, it is best to ask the group if they would like to stop, debrief, and/or pray for the person who is sharing or for their family member.

4. Imagine that Chris is a high school student who has attended your church since before he was born. He has recently made it public that he is gay. Lately, you've heard some of the other students making fun of him at church. You've also heard some of the parents saying that they don't want him to go on the church retreat and room with their sons. Which issue do you think is a priority and why? If you

have time in your group, discuss how you would handle each situation.

5. Imagine an LGBT support group has recently formed at the local school. One local church wants to ban it for what they feel are moral reasons. Another church wants to have it funded by the school district, with the hope that it will help stop the bullying of LGBT students. Where do you stand between the two churches? If you don't agree with either, what's an alternative set of actions you would propose?

Scripture Discussion ─────────────────

1. Read Matthew 19:13 – 14, Mark 10:13 – 16, and Luke 18:15 – 17. In these passages, notice the following:

   How does the community respond to Jesus?

   What is the disciples' reaction to the children and why?

   How does Jesus show value toward the children? Why do you think children are so important to him?

   What principles can we take from those passages and apply to today's LGBT youth?

2. Although the Bible doesn't talk specifically about bullying, it does have many passages that talk about how God
   defends those who are oppressed. Examine the following verses and write down a response to them: Psalm 9:9;
   Psalm 146:7; Isaiah 1:17; Isaiah 10:1–2; Luke 4:18–19.

How do these verses apply to LGBT adolescents today?

Wrap-Up

If your group has time, watch another story from the Real
Stories section of the DVD.

In the main video presentation, Andrew talks about a
conversation he had with a man who prayed that God would
change him. Many LGBT adolescents struggle not only with
how their peers and family perceive them but with how they
think God perceives them. Read Psalm 42 through the eyes of
an LGBT adolescent. Then pray for the lesbian, gay, bisexual,
and transgender adolescents in your community and in your
church. No matter if you agree or disagree with them, you can
validate the difficult road to be traversed at such a vulnerable
time for any youth.

Next Steps

Choose one of the following steps to further explore the session topic or to act on what you've learned. You may want to keep a journal of the steps you take, or discuss them in your group gathering.

1. Bullying is a deeply concerning issue among LGBT youth. Develop a plan for your group and/or church to respond to this issue both internally and in the local community.

2. Explore what resources your surrounding community has for LGBT adolescents. Consider health care, counseling, support groups, homeless shelters, and pastoral care. Develop a list for your church and other faith communities in your vicinity, and work to partner with them to make a tangible impact in such an important area of need.

3. Have a conversation with some LGBT adolescents and ask them about their experiences at school, in church, and with their family and friends. Ask them what resources or services they would like to see the church provide to the LGBT adolescents in your community.

4. Search some of the websites listed in the resource section that follows on pages 74–75. Note the main issues that LGBT adolescents face. Also note some of the issues of their family members. How might the church help meet any of those needs?

Resources

Inclusion on this list should not be seen as an endorsement of an organization, nor should exclusion of any organization be seen as a rejection. Their mission statements are from their websites.

The Ali Forney Center: Housing for the Homeless LGBT Youth

www.aliforneycenter.org

Their mission: "Our mission is to protect LGBTQ youth from the harm of homelessness, and to support them in becoming safe and independent as they move from adolescence to adulthood."

Gay, Lesbian and Straight Education Network/GLSEN

www.glsen.org

Their mission: "The Gay, Lesbian & Straight Education Network strives to assure that each member of every school community is valued and respected regardless of sexual orientation or gender identity/expression."

It Gets Better Project

www.itgetsbetter.org

Their description: "The website *www.itgetsbetter.org* is a place where young people who are lesbian, gay, bi, or trans can see how love and happiness can be a reality in their future. It's a place where our straight allies can visit and support their friends and family members. It's a place where people can share their stories, take the It Gets Better Project pledge, watch videos of love and support, and seek help through the Trevor Project and GLSEN."

Matthew Shepard Foundation
www.matthewshepard.org
Their mission: "To support diversity programs in education and to help youth organizations establish environments where young people can feel safe and be themselves.

Stop Bullying
www.stopbullying.gov
Their mission: "*StopBullying.gov* provides information from various government agencies on how kids, teens, young adults, parents, educators and others in the community can prevent or stop bullying." They have a special section on LGBT bullying: *www.stopbullying.gov/topics/lgbt/*.

The Trevor Project
www.thetrevorproject.org
Their mission: "The Trevor Project is determined to end suicide among LGBTQ youth by providing life-saving and life-affirming resources including our nationwide, 24/7 crisis intervention lifeline, digital community and advocacy/educational programs that create a safe, supportive and positive environment for everyone."

Living in the Tension

But I must confess that I am not afraid of the word "tension." I have earnestly opposed violent tension, but there is a type of constructive, nonviolent tension which is necessary for growth. Just as Socrates felt that it was necessary to create a tension in the mind so that individuals could rise from the bondage of myths and half-truths to the unfettered realm of creative analysis and objective appraisal, we must see the need for nonviolent gadflies to create the kind of tension in society that will help men rise from the dark depths of prejudice and racism to the majestic heights of understanding and brotherhood.

(Martin Luther King Jr.,
Letter from a Birmingham Jail, April 16, 1963)

What Is a Living in the Tension Gathering?

Living in the Tension gatherings are for people of all different shades of faith and sexuality in our culture today—secular LGBT, Christian LGBT, ex-gay, celibate, Christian heterosexual (liberal and conservative), and non-Christian heterosexual—to willfully enter into a place of constructive tension, intentionally forming a community that peacefully and productively takes on the most divisive topics within the culture war that is faith and sexuality. It's what we call our Holy Uncomfortableness (*www.themarinfoundation.org*).

Starter Question —————————————————————————————

How do you typically respond when you are involved in an uncomfortable conversation?

Video Teaching Session #6 ———————

Use the following outline to follow along with the video or take notes if you wish.

Dr. Martin Luther King Jr. quotation

Constructive tension

Commit. Stay. Reconcile. Grow.

Commit

Stay

Reconcile

Grow

Characteristics of Living in the Tension gatherings

Ground rules of Living in the Tension gatherings

1.   We're not here to convince anybody of anything.

2.   Everybody's story is legitimate to them.

3.   Everybody needs to talk.

Structure of a Living in the Tension gathering

Part 1. Introduction

Part 2. The conversation

Part 3. The way forward

Video Discussion

1. How do you typically respond when someone disagrees with your point of view? Check the answer that best describes you.

   ❑ I try to argue the point so they will come to agree with me.

   ❑ I shut down and try to remove myself from the conversation.

   ❑ I try to divert the conversation to a less-disagreeable topic.

   ❑ I try to listen to their point of view in order to understand how they arrived there.

   Would a close friend or family member agree with your response? Why do you think you usually deal with conflicts as you do? Is there anything you might want to change about your typical response method?

2. Following are two situations that may raise tension in your church. Consider not only how you might respond, but how you would educate the church in regard to the issue raised.

   • Someone starts attending your church who is transgender. This person has asked the pastor which bathroom to use, and the pastor has come to you for advice. What would you say? (The "Transgender at Work" website offers some advice that may be applicable to the church: *www.tgender.net/taw/restroom.html.*)

- Jon and his partner, Robert, have been together for over fifteen years and have adopted three children. Both of them have become Christians over the past year and are looking for a church in which to raise their family. What kind of response would they receive from your church? Are you satisfied with that response or would you challenge the church to respond differently?

Scripture Discussion ————————————

1. The Bible is full of examples of people in tension with each other. One of the most notable in the New Testament is Acts 15:1–35, where two different perspectives are being taught about salvation. Read these verses; then answer the following questions:

   What is the nature of the tension and who are the parties at odds?

What steps are taken to resolve the conflict?

What kingdom principles can we learn from this interaction?

How can we apply them to our work building bridges with the LGBT community?

2. Another example of tension is found in Galatians 2, where Peter and Paul are in conflict. Read the chapter with the following questions in mind:

   What is the essence of the disagreement between Peter and Paul?

   Why do you think Paul may have confronted Peter in front of others?

How was this tension resolved?

What are some kingdom principles we can take from this chapter and apply to our work of building bridges with the LGBT community?

LEADER TIPS

1. As the study concludes, be sure to review what people have learned: insights they have had and steps they have taken. Spend time celebrating the group's achievements and growth.

2. Talk about how to continue the learning process after the group ends. How will group members continue to learn about and, most importantly, engage the LGBT community and continue to build bridges?

3. Pray for each other and the stories you have heard during the time you've been together as a group.

Wrap-Up

If your group has time, watch another story from the Real Stories section of the DVD.

As you draw this study to a close, thank God for the people in the group and what you've learned together. Ask God to continue to give you opportunities to build bridges with the LGBT community and for courage to live in the tension for the sake of the kingdom we so boldly proclaim to live within.

Next Steps

Choose one of the following steps to further explore the session topic or to act on what you've learned. You may want to keep a journal of the steps you take, or discuss them in a future group gathering.

1. Consider the examples of topics (Appendix B, beginning on page 91) that The Marin Foundation has used for their Living in the Tension gatherings. Have your group choose one topic and plan a gathering in the next three months.
2. Choose one of the topics listed in Appendix B to research more fully. Write up a brief description of your findings and discuss it with members of your group.
3. Consider all the action steps you've taken throughout this study. Is there one step you've been hesitant to take? Write it down, talk to your group about it, ask God for the courage to take that step, and then go take it! Afterward, report back to your group to reflect on your experience.

Website Resources

This is only a small selection of the many organizations that pertain to homosexuality. Inclusion on this list should not be seen as an endorsement of an organization, nor should exclusion of any organization be seen as a rejection. Mission statements/descriptions are taken from their websites. More resources regarding LGBT adolescents are found at the end of Session 5.

General

The Marin Foundation
www.themarinfoundation.org
Their mission: "The Marin Foundation is a 501(c)/(3) non-profit that works to build bridges between the LGBT community and the church through scientific research, biblical and social education, and diverse community gatherings."

Gay Christian Network
www.gaychristian.net
Their mission: "The Gay Christian Network (GCN) is a nonprofit ministry supporting Christians worldwide who happen to be lesbian, gay, bisexual, or transgender (LGBT). Our mission, 'sharing Christ's light and love for all,' is carried out in five primary directions, to impact individuals, families, communities, churches, and the world."

New Direction Ministries of Canada
www.newdirection.ca
Their mission: "Nurturing safe and spacious places for those outside the heterosexual mainstream to explore and grow in faith in Jesus Christ."

Procon.org
www.procon.org
Their mission: "Promoting critical thinking, education, and informed citizenship by presenting controversial issues in a straightforward, nonpartisan, primarily pro-con format." Procon.org presents research on 42 issues. Two issues specific to homosexuality:

- "Born Gay"
  http://borngay.procon.org/view.answers.php?questionID=001335
- "Gay Marriage"
  http://gaymarriage.procon.org/

Progressive

These organizations are more likely to advocate for a historically pro-LGBT perspective. They range from what would generally be viewed as mildly to strongly progressive.

COLAGE: People with a Lesbian, Gay, Bisexual, Transgender, or Queer Parent
www.colage.org
COLAGE is a national movement of children, youth, and adults with one or more lesbian, gay, bisexual, transgender, and/or queer (LGBTQ) parents. "We build community and work toward social justice through youth empowerment, leadership development, education, and advocacy."

Gay & Lesbian Alliance Against Defamation/GLAAD
www.glaad.org

Their mission: "GLAAD amplifies the voice of the LGBT community by empowering real people to share their stories, holding the media accountable for the words and images they present, and helping grassroots organizations communicate effectively. By ensuring that the stories of LGBT people are heard through the media, GLAAD promotes understanding, increases acceptance, and advances equality."

GLBTQ.com
www.glbtq.com

Their description: "*Glbtq.com* is the largest website devoted to gay, lesbian, bisexual, transgender, and queer (GLBTQ) education and culture and houses the largest, most comprehensive encyclopedia of GLBTQ culture in the world."

Intersex Society of North America/ISNA
www.isna.org

Their mission: "The Intersex Society of North America (ISNA) is devoted to systemic change to end shame, secrecy, and unwanted genital surgeries for people born with an anatomy that someone decided is not standard for male or female."

NOTE: ISNA closed operations in 2008. However, the website is left up as "historical artifact" and has a helpful cache of resources. They have been replaced by Accord Alliance (*www.accordalliance.org*), an organization that addresses disorders of sex development.

Parents, Families and Friends of Lesbians and Gays/PFLAG
www.pflag.org

Their mission: "PFLAG promotes the health and well-being of lesbian, gay, bisexual and transgender persons, their families and friends through: support, to cope with an adverse society; education, to enlighten an ill-informed public; and advocacy, to end discrimination and to secure equal civil rights. Parents, Families and Friends of Lesbians and Gays provides opportunity for dialogue about sexual orientation and gender identity, and acts to create a society that is healthy and respectful of human diversity."

Soulforce
www.soulforce.org
Their mission: "Soulforce is committed to relentless nonviolent resistance to bring freedom to lesbian, gay, bisexual, transgender, and queer people from religious and political oppression."

Conservative ————————————————————————

These organizations are more likely to advocate for a historically conservative LGBT perspective. They range from what would be generally viewed as mildly to strongly conservative.

Citizens for Community Values
www.ccv.org
Their mission: "Citizens for Community Values (CCV) exists to promote Judeo-Christian moral values, and to reduce destructive behaviors contrary to those values, through education, active community partnership, and individual empowerment at the local, state and national levels."

NOTE: CCV focuses on a number of issues. This is the link to their perspective on homosexuality: *www.ccv.org/issues/homosexuality/*.

Exodus International
http://exodusinternational.org/
Their mission: "Mobilizing the body of Christ to minister grace and truth to a world impacted by homosexuality."

Living in the Tension Guide

For the full downloadable PDF of the Living in the Tension Guide that includes the following additional information:

- purpose
- mission statement
- need
- ground rules
- structure
- locations
- frequency
- how to build, grow, and sustain a Living in the Tension group
- and more

please visit *http://www.themarinfoundation.org/resources/love-is-an-orientation-dvd-curriculum/.*

Following you will find an alphabetical list of some topics that The Marin Foundation has used over the last couple of years in our own Living in the Tension gatherings. Each topic includes a brief summary and a couple sample questions or thoughts to assist you in starting to think about the big idea of each gathering and how you can engage your group in the most transparent ways possible.

Activism

Old paradigms of engagement (e.g., large group gatherings, marches, protests) are dwindling in their effectiveness of influencing national policy. How is this new generation changing the old "acceptable medium of engagement" and where is activism heading? What does it look like to instill a new medium of engagement in our own lives as well as in broader culture?

Bullying

There has been a string of LGBT teenage suicides recently. Who in your group has been bullied (whether LGBT or not), how did they respond, what are the effects, and what can we do about it?

Celibacy

Though very countercultural to the mainstream, celibacy is a means of commitment to a traditional orthodox view of Scripture for those with a same-sex attraction. What is it like to be "alone" for a lifetime, not being able to engage in what most Christians believe to be the God-given gift of human sexuality?

Change

What is change? Is it behavior modification or something else? Is it mandatory for Christians? What about partnered gay Christians? What if people never "change"? Has anyone ever gone through reparative therapy? What was the experience like? What about the outcome?

Conflict

How are we to handle conflict? Is it different coming from Christians versus coming from non-Christians? What does it look like to bring reconciliation amid divisive conflicts and accusations?

Current Social Issues

Pick a current social issue related to homosexuality and run with it. Some examples: the anti-homosexual bill in Uganda, gay adoption legislation, the military's "don't ask, don't tell" policy.

Day of Silence

The Day of Silence occurs April 15th every year, when LGBT students and their friends don't speak all day in school to bring light to the general oppression of LGBT youth. Commit to not speaking at all that day and at the gathering talk about silence, death, reflection, oppression, and finding your voice.

Deconstruction of Cultural Labels, Socially Constructed Boxes, and the Influence Those Labels Yield

Many times cultural stereotypes become the "generalizable" label assigned to a certain group of people. Such a distinction has a lasting influence and can lead to a destructive path of self-fulfilling prophecies. Just because culture might see a stereotype or label as acceptable doesn't mean it's correct or biblical. What is a gay Christian? Are there different types? What about evangelicals? How have culturally accepted perceptions negatively impacted bridge-building relationships and how do we usher in a more nuanced paradigm of engagement?

Elevating the Conversation

It is too easy to get caught up in a continual cycle of fighting about the same social, political, theological, and scientific issues. What does it mean to elevate such divisiveness to broader principles that elongate the conversation and build bridges through commitment?

Engaging in Sex

What is sex? Who defines it? Who has had it? Who hasn't? What influence or pressure does it yield over you? How does it (or not) define you, your relationships, and your future?

Fidelity

Does friendship evangelism betray the friendship because there is a preconceived "outcome" already in place? What does it mean to have someone's back no matter what? How have such experiences influenced worldviews, culture wars, and this group? When have you stood with someone and taken heat for them when it wasn't even your place to do so?

Forgiveness

There are a lot of people to hate in this world for a whole lot of reasons—personally and corporately. Is it important to forgive? What does that look like and what is the process to forgive? Is it easy or hard? Is it a single act or a lifestyle? How have you personally experienced or not experienced forgiveness in your life?

Free Will

What does free will have to do with making choices about faith, sex, and life? Is free will an excuse or is it a driving force to make things better? How does free will play into "change" or the decision to be partnered or celibate? Which is justified?

Gay Marriage

How do you see a resolution to the fight concerning gay marriage? What would your suggestions be for the future outcome our country adopts? Also, though many Christians look at this as a singular moral issue, there are two other components that involve the broader debate of church and state:

Human Rights

Do two LGBT consenting American adults deserve the same rights as two straight consenting American adults?

Legal Rights

Do two LGBT consenting American adults deserve the

same benefits (insurance, etc.) and tax and legal breaks as two straight consenting American adults?

Guilt and Regret

What does guilt or regret look like in your own life, either in the "big picture" or in sexual relationships, and what are you supposed to do about it?

Handling Critics

We will always have critics. How are we supposed to respond to them? What examples might you share from your own life? What is the difference between a critique, criticism, and a display of hatred? Does the Bible say anything about this topic?

HIV/AIDS

Every day there are 7,000 new HIV infections around the world. How has this truth impacted your life, and what are you doing about it? What about the perception and stigma of LGBT people with HIV/AIDS, especially in a church context?

Hooking Up

Yes, even good Christians hook up. Is there a "too far"? Are there take-backs? What, if anything, separates sexuality from hooking up?

I'm Sorry

There is power in those words. What times have you said "I'm sorry" that have impacted you and another person more than either of you ever thought?

Intersex

Ever wonder what it is like to not know what bathroom to walk into? What about the faith journey of someone who from birth is genetically both male and female? Watch the interview at *www.loveisanorientation.com/2010/video-of-living-in-the-tension-event-intersex/* and then discuss.

Language, Words, Biases, and Stereotypes that Tear Us Down

Listen to each others' stories and the emotional, spiritual, and mental impact those experiences have had on us. How do you break down these walls to build the wounded back up?

Love Is an Orientation

Andrew Marin's book, *Love Is an Orientation*, has 11 chapters, including the conclusion, with a total of 78 subheadings that explore a variety of issues surrounding faith, sexuality, and bridge building. Each of those subheadings can be used as a starting point for Living in the Tension gatherings, using Andrew's thoughts as a baseline to agree/disagree/discuss around.

Love Your Enemies

There is no more countercultural command by Jesus than this one. Though many people cognitively understand the concept of loving one's enemies, what does it actually look like and how has it (if it has at all) played out in your life?

Movies

Watch the following movies during different gatherings and then discuss them: *Milk* (gay rights), *I Do Exist* (ex-gay), *Stonewall Uprising* (LGBT history), *Paris Is Burning* (transgender).

National Coming Out Day

National Coming Out Day, which occurs October 11th every year, is the time to hear people's stories of publicly proclaiming their sexual orientation and to live in the emotion of it all. For those who are not LGBT or have not come out, it's important to confess something that no one else knows about you.

Normal/Normalcy

What is normal? Who is normal? What defines normalcy in today's culture in all areas of your life and broader society?

Perceptions that Influence Your Reality

There are number of very negative perceptions about the LGBT community (e.g., they were abused or raped as youth, party all the time, will get infected with HIV or STDS, etc.) as well as a number of very negative perceptions about Christians (e.g., they are anti-gay, judgmental, hypocritical, etc.). What do these mean to your life and how have they influenced you, your own perception of your community and others, and how you treat "the other" based on what you think they think about you?

Personal Journeys from All Shades of Faith and Sexuality

Bring in guests to share their experiences about faith and sexuality (also from different ethnicities and genders if possible) and then have an open Q & A. Example speakers would be:

- Non-Christian LGBT person
- Gay Christian
- Bisexual person (believer/non-believer)
- Transgender person (believer/non-believer)
- Partnered/married LGBTs (with/without kids and believer/non)
- Celibate person with a same-sex attraction
- Ex-gay person
- Liberal straight Christian (lay person and pastor)
- Conservative straight Christian (lay person and pastor)
- Non-Christian straight person
- Local politician

- University administrator
- CEO or HR person from a for-profit business

Power Structures

Certain cultural hierarchies give power and access, influence power and access, or take away power and access from others. How do those structures influence your life/sexuality/faith and how can you subvert them to make an individual and cultural impact?

Pride Parade

Pride parades are traditionally held the last weekend in June every year to commemorate the Stonewall Riots—what historians call the first ever public "outing" of the LGBT community. Speak about the social and political history of the LGBT movement, where it is now, and where it is going.

Prop 8

How does faith influence politics, and is that right or wrong? Who actually "won" the recent Prop 8 vote—not necessarily by votes but by impact?

Race and Ethnic Relations Surrounding Sexuality

Different ethnicities treat (homo)sexuality differently. What have you experienced and what is a way forward?

Reconciliation

There is a difference between *cultural reconciliation* (you believe what I believe, then we'll be reconciled) and *actual reconciliation* (relentlessly pursuing those people most unlike ourselves, connecting on a human-to-human level with our differences). From a Christian perspective, we can achieve actual reconciliation because that is what our Savior modeled for us. What are the theological, social, political, and scientific means by which we can live out an actual reconciliation?

Research

Myth or fact? Research today is used as a political tool to wield power. Some research says LGBT persons are born that way; other research says they're not. What do you believe about that and a number of other differing statistics; and how can we move forward through the clear opposition?

Role Play

Role-play scenes and stereotypes of the common back-and-forth arguments between the LGBT community and conservatives. Yell. Get upset. Keep it real. Practice applications of real-time responses and elevating the conversation in the heat of the moment.

Service in the Community

Instead of always talking or watching, it is important to get out in your community as a group and serve together. The Marin Foundation tries to plan a few community service projects a year to be and work together as one body making a tangible difference.

Separation between Church and State

What does this separation look like and how does it actually play out in our church and mainstream cultures? What are its ramifications for theological and political issues?

Sexual Identity

Why do we identify sexually as we do? What is the basis of identity? What defines us—actions, sex, faith, politics? Are any of those intertwined or more important than the others?

Sexual Orientation

What is sexual orientation, whether gay or straight? Does it matter? What does the Bible say about sexual orientation?

How does sexual orientation define/influence your life, thoughts, faith, and sexuality?

Scriptures about Homosexuality

There are six main passages in the Bible that reference same-sex sexual behavior. People can argue all day about the Greek, Hebrew, and historical cultural contexts surrounding each passage. Go through each passage presenting *both* the "pro-gay" theological argument and the conservative theological argument. Listen to and learn from each, not as a tool for changing convictions, but as one that sees "the other" theology as a legitimate expression of where that belief system is coming from.

Sin

What is sin? How is it defined? It is the most politically incorrect word in our society. How does faith and sexuality encompass this? What are the overarching principles surrounding a doctrine of sin? How can each of you relate to sin, faith, and sexuality?

Shame

There is an immense amount of shame and disconnect associated with being in the closet. Whether LGBT or not, what are you ashamed about (if anything)? Let it out. What was it like before? How has it stuck with you and shaped you?

Solidarity

What does it mean to stand with someone oppressed— faith-wise or sexually?

Trust

Where does trust come from, how does one earn it, and what happens when it is lost?

Validation vs. Affirmation

There is a difference between these two constructs. What is it and how can you implement this difference in practical applications that foster actual reconciliation?

Yes/No

Twenty-two of twenty-five times recorded in Scripture, Jesus did not answer yes or no to the yes-no questions asked of him — whether asked by his enemies (fifteen times) or his friends (ten times). For more in-depth analysis, reference pages 103–105 and 178–185 in Andrew Marin's book, *Love Is an Orientation*.

Leader Tips

Group Guidelines

Establish group guidelines when the group first starts. It is better to do this at the beginning than to wait until conversations become heated. Review them at the beginning of every gathering.

Examples:

- *Use "I," not "we," when speaking.* This guideline helps people in the group speak only for themselves and not others; e.g., "I think that ..." versus "We think that...." By using "we," a person can intentionally or unintentionally create a false sense that many people agree with their perspective. This can become divisive as it turns into a "we versus them" argument.
- *Allow people to speak without interrupting or interpreting what they are saying.* People are sharing personal information. Honor that by not allowing other people to interrupt. Caveat: If you have a long-winded speaker, you may need to set a time frame for sharing. For example, "Each person has two minutes to share their next steps." Have a timer ready so to be fair.
- *Ask for a certain level of confidentiality.* It is impossible to guarantee confidentiality in a group setting. However, you can ask the group participants to honor each other

by not repeating anyone else's story or responses outside of the group.

Handling Discussion of Controversial Topics

The topic of homosexuality has the potential to be very volatile. As a group leader, you set the pace and the tone of the discussion. It is important that you remember that your role is to facilitate, not to preach. Here are some tips to help you:

1. *Encourage participants to have the stance of a learner.* In his book, *Cross-Cultural Servanthood* (InterVarsity Press, 2006), Duane Elmer makes this observation: "The first skill necessary for developing an attitude of openness toward others who are different is the ability to suspend judgment." When we judge, we stop learning because we've come to a conclusion and don't need any more information. Seek to help the participants continue to learn about this topic.

2. *Deal with people who have an agenda early on in the group's life.* You may need to pull them aside before the gathering even begins and have an honest conversation. It might go something like this: "I know you have strong thoughts about this topic, but this discussion is about building bridges. If you start speaking without listening to others or become argumentative or antagonistic, I will ask you to stop. I will do so respectfully, but I will do it."

3. *Challenge people to talk **to** people, not **at** them.* Sometimes when people have strong opinions about a topic, they think the more they talk, the better their chances are

of convincing the other party to see their point of view. Encourage a "no preaching" policy.

4. *Be sensitive to the emotional climate of the group.* It is highly likely that at least one person in the group has a personal connection to the topic. Be aware of people's emotional reactions: increased nervousness, outbursts of anger, shutting down, or becoming extremely quiet.

5. *Don't be afraid of conflict and tension.* If a group is to talk deeply about a topic and be committed to each other, it is important that they learn how to handle difficult conversations. Don't shut down a heated debate unless it becomes hurtful. Seek to help group members come to a healthy resolution before the group dismisses. Scott Peck has some helpful advice in his book *The Different Drum: Community Making and Peace* (Touchstone, 1998). A condensed version can be found here: *http://fce-community.org/stages-of-cb/.*

6. *Pray.* Homosexuality and faith is a difficult topic for many people. It is vital that, as a leader, you pray as the group is forming, as well as before you lead each session. Weave prayer throughout the group discussion as well, being sensitive to what is appropriate in that culture.

Follow-Up

The Marin Foundation hopes that the *Love Is an Orientation* video curriculum gives you a solid starting point that sets you on the right path to building bridges between the LGBT and conservative Christian communities. When you work to build a bridge, you make yourself vulnerable to get walked on by both sides. That, however, is part of the countercultural boldness that comes with living in the tension of the most divisive topic in our culture today. If your university, seminary, church, organization, or group would like to talk with, ask questions of, or partner with our work, or schedule us for a speaking engagement, please contact us at *info@themarinfoundation.org*.

Again, thank you for your willingness to engage this curriculum and to make an impact in your local community. Much love.

The Marin Foundation
5241 N. Ashland Avenue, 1st Floor
Chicago, IL 60640
Office Phone: 773.572.5983
Email: *info@themarinfoundation.org*
Web: *www.themarinfoundation.org*
Blog: *www.loveisanorientation.com*
Facebook: *www.facebook.com/TheMarinFoundation*
Twitter: @MarinFoundation or @Andrew_Marin

Also Available from
InterVarsity Press

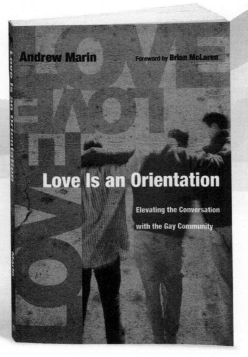

978-0-8308-**3626**-0, Paperback, 205 pages

Discounts Available on Bulk Orders

To order, please visit **www.ivpress.com/loveisanorientation**

or call **1-800-843-9487.**

Use the following coupon code when ordering: **506-307**

(U.S. orders only)

Share Your Thoughts

With the Author: Your comments will be forwarded to
the author when you send them to *zauthor@zondervan.com*.

With Zondervan: Submit your review of this book
by writing to *zreview@zondervan.com*.

Free Online Resources at
www.zondervan.com

Zondervan AuthorTracker: Be notified whenever your favorite
authors publish new books, go on tour, or post an update
about what's happening in their lives at www.zondervan.com/
authortracker.

Daily Bible Verses and Devotions: Enrich your life with daily
Bible verses or devotions that help you start every morning
focused on God. Visit www.zondervan.com/newsletters.

Free Email Publications: Sign up for newsletters on Christian
living, academic resources, church ministry, fiction, children's
resources, and more. Visit www.zondervan.com/newsletters.

Zondervan Bible Search: Find and compare Bible passages in
a variety of translations at www.zondervanbiblesearch.com.

Other Benefits: Register yourself to receive online benefits
like coupons and special offers, or to participate in research.

ZONDERVAN®

ZONDERVAN.com/
AUTHORTRACKER
follow your favorite authors